NARWHAL

Unicorn of the Sea

SMITHSONIAN OCEANIC COLLECTION

With lots of love to my grandson, Benji, who loves a good story.—J.H.

To KathyAnn, Stephanie and Christopher with all my love for all their support.—S.J.P.

Book copyright © 2008 Trudy Corporation,
and the Smithsonian Institution, Washington, DC 20560.

Published by Soundprints, an imprint of Trudy Corporation, Norwalk, Connecticut.
www.soundprints.com

Series design: Shields & Partners, Westport, CT
Editor: Barbie Heit Schwaeber
Book layout: Katie Sears
Production coordinator: Chris Dobias
Audio design: Brian E. Giblin

First Edition 2008
10 9 8 7 6 5 4 3 2 1
Printed in China

Acknowledgments:
    Janet Halfmann would like to thank Dr. Kristin Laidre of the Polar Science Center at the University of Washington in Seattle for answering many questions about narwhals and their habitat.
    Steven James Petruccio wishes to acknowledge the curators at the Smithsonian Institution for helping make this book as accurate as it is interesting. He gives thanks to Barbie Heit Schwaeber for allowing the necessary time and resources to create this book and to Katie Sears for ensuring high art and design standards.
    Soundprints gives very special thanks to Dr. Don E. Wilson of the Division of Mammals: Department of Vertebrate Zoology at the Smithsonian Institution's National Museum of Natural History for his curatorial review. We would also like to thank Ellen Nanney at the Smithsonian Institution's Office of Product Development and Licensing for her help in the creation of this book.

Library of Congress Cataloging-in-Publication Data

Halfmann, Janet.

Narwhal unicorn of the sea/by Janet Halfmann; illustrated by Steven James Petruccio.—1st ed.
    p. cm.—(Smithsonian oceanic collection)
ISBN 978-1-59249-868-0 (hardcover book)—ISBN 978-1-59249-869-7 (micro book)—ISBN 978-1-59249-870-3 (pbk. book)
1. Narwhal—Arctic regions—Juvenile literature. I. Petruccio, Steven, ill. II. Title.
QL737.C433H35 2008
599.5'43—dc22
                    2008017120

NARWHAL
Unicorn of the Sea

by Janet Halfmann   Illustrated by Steven James Petruccio

"*Tuugaalik, tuugaalik!* Narwhal, narwhal!" shout the Inuit children standing on the shore. The bright all-day sun of July is breaking up the ice in the inlets and bays of Canada's high Arctic. Narwhal is returning from the sea to his summer home near land. Hundreds of other narwhals travel with him.

5

Narwhal has made this long journey many times before. He was born in these coastal waters twelve summers ago.

Now it is another summer, and more baby narwhals are being born. The new calves are big, just as Narwhal was, in order to survive in these cold waters near the North Pole. The pale gray babies drink milk underwater from their spotted mothers. Then, tummies full, it's time for nudging and rolling games with Mom.

At twelve years old, Narwhal is grown up, with a long, spiral tooth sticking out like a unicorn horn from his upper jaw. He crosses teeth with other males, as though gently jousting to be king of the sea. *Clickety, clack!* The teeth tap like wooden drumsticks.

One morning, a tourist boat appears in a bay where Narwhal's pod is resting. Narwhal "stands" in the water and pokes out his head to sneak a peak at the boat.

Men, women and children point at him. Shy of people, Narwhal quickly dives beneath the shimmering blue water. When he finally comes up to breathe, the boat has left, attracted by ringed seals across the bay.

That evening, other visitors slide into the bay. Six tall black fins slice the water. A pod of killer whales is prowling for dinner.

Narwhal hears one of the killer whales call to a teammate. Instantly, Narwhal and his podmates fall silent. Terrified, they flee to a shallow area of the bay. Crowded together in the shadows, they lie motionless, barely breathing.

The killer whales cruise near, but to them the narwhals look like floating pieces of ice. The killer whales listen, but hear nothing. Finally, they give up and leave to look for food elsewhere.

Soon the brief Arctic summer is over. Days grow shorter and cooler. Seabirds and songbirds fly south to warmer places. Ice begins to form in the inlets and bays.

In mid-September, before Narwhal's summer waters freeze solid and trap him, he heads toward the sea. There, watery cracks stay open all winter between the huge sheets of drifting ice, creating places where he can come up for air.

On the way to the sea, Narwhal and his podmates get hungry. They stop in an inlet teeming with fish. Diving again and again, they stuff themselves with cod for the long trip.

That night, an early winter storm hits the inlet. The temperature plunges. By morning, a mile-wide band of thick ice blocks the entrance to the inlet. The narwhals are trapped inside.

19

For three days, they nervously swim and dive, searching for a way out. On the fourth morning, polar bears find the icy prison. Crouching on the ice, they silently wait for the trapped narwhals to surface for air.

But the narwhals are already gone. Rising temperatures during the night created a narrow crack of water out of the inlet. Once more, the narwhals are swimming toward the sea.

Narwhal reaches his winter home in November, during the long polar night when the sun never shines. The wind howls and the ice creaks. But Narwhal is comfortable and warm in a thick layer of blubber. And he knows that far beneath the ice swim thousands of his favorite fish.

Arching his finless back, he easily dives beneath the ice, straight down to the bottom of the deep, dark sea. He sucks up flatfish after flatfish, swallowing them whole.

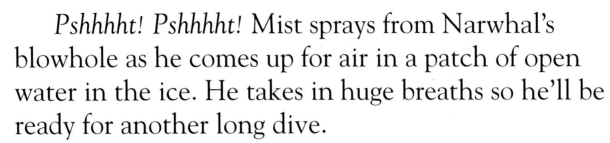

Pshhhht! Pshhhht! Mist sprays from Narwhal's blowhole as he comes up for air in a patch of open water in the ice. He takes in huge breaths so he'll be ready for another long dive.

Narwhal is not alone in this dark frozen world beneath the North Star. From time to time, he sees bowhead whales, polar bears, walruses, bearded seals and ringed seals. But no killer whales bother him here—their tall back fins would get in the way under the ice.

Sometimes, beautiful northern lights dance across the sky, rippling in curtains of red, green and blue.

As the weeks pass and winter winds blow colder, open areas of water for breathing become smaller and smaller.

Bam! Bam! Narwhal bashes his head against the icy edges of a patch of open water. His podmates bump the ice, too. They all work until they're exhausted. But their precious breathing hole in the ice stays open.

Life at the top of the world is not easy. But to Narwhal it is home.
All through the cold, dark winter, he'll keep diving and fishing,
as his ancestors have done for hundreds of thousands of years.
Come spring, he'll journey toward land once again. And in July,
Inuit children will cheer, *"Tuugaalik, tuugaalik!"*

About the Narwhal

The narwhal is a small whale that lives its entire life in the Arctic. Like all whales, the narwhal is a mammal, not a fish. The male has a long tooth that juts out nine feet from its upper left jaw. The female only rarely has the tooth. Scientists are not sure of the tooth's purpose. In 2005, a team of scientists headed by a dentist discovered that a narwhal's tooth is very sensitive, with millions of nerve endings exposed to the cold. So it is likely that the tooth is sensing the narwhal's environment, such as when water is about to freeze. Much about the narwhal is still unknown because of the difficulty of studying it in its dark winter home in the drifting sea ice.

In ages past, traders sold narwhal teeth as unicorn horns, for as much as ten times their weight in gold. Even today, narwhal teeth are highly prized, earning hunters large sums of money.

There are about 80,000 narwhals. Most spend the winter in the drifting ice, called pack ice, of Baffin Bay and Davis Strait between northeast Canada and Greenland. In summer, the narwhals migrate hundreds of miles north to high Arctic coasts of Canada and Greenland.

Narwhals grow about fifteen feet long, with females shorter. They mate in April in the pack ice, and the calves are born fifteen months later in summer coastal waters. Most narwhals live less than thirty years.

Narwhals can dive more than a mile to catch fish and can stay underwater for thirty minutes—an amazing feat. They hunt daily during the winter and often while traveling, but eat little in summer waters. They eat flatfish, cod, squid and shrimp.

The Inuit hunt the narwhal for its tusk, meat and skin, which is high in Vitamin C. Recently, narwhals have been helping scientists learn about climate change in the Arctic. Devices placed on the animals measure the winter water temperature between Greenland and Canada 400 times a day.

Glossary

Arctic: Area around the North Pole where it is very cold; winter days have 24 hours of darkness and summer days have 24 hours of sunlight.

blowhole: A nostril on the top of a whale's head.

blubber: Thick layer of fat under a whale's skin.

Inuit: Native people of the Arctic; the word means "The People."

migrate: To move on a regular basis from one place to another.

northern lights: Bands or rays of moving light sometimes seen in the northern sky at night.

North Pole: Point on the earth that is farthest north.

North Star: A bright star in the northern sky above the North Pole.

pod: A group of whales.

polar night: The months of darkness during the Arctic winter.

unicorn: An imaginary animal that looks like a white horse with a long pointed horn in the middle of its forehead. In legendary tales, the horn is thought to have special powers.

Points of Interest in this Book